W9-BFY-036

5/14

RARE AND PRECIOUS
METALS

GOLD

By Therese Shea

Gareth Stevens
Publishing

Please visit our website, www.garethstevens.com. For a free color catalog of all our high-quality books, call toll free 1-800-542-2595 or fax 1-877-542-2596.

Library of Congress Cataloging-in-Publication Data

Shea, Therese.
Gold / by Therese Shea.
 p. cm. — (Rare and precious metals)
Includes index.
ISBN 978-1-4824-0503-3 (library binding) —
ISBN 978-1-4824-0500-2 (pbk.) —
ISBN 978-1-4824-0501-9 (6-pack)
1. Gold — Juvenile literature. I. Shea, Therese. II. Title.
QD181.A9 S54 2014
669.22—dc23

First Edition

Published in 2014 by
Gareth Stevens Publishing
111 East 14th Street, Suite 349
New York, NY 10003

Copyright © 2014 Gareth Stevens Publishing

Designer: Nicholas Domiano
Editor: Therese Shea

Photo credits: Cover, p. 1 optimarc/Shutterstock.com; pp. 3-24 (inset graphic) Aleksandr Bryliaev/Shutterstock.com; pp. 3-24 (caption box) Hemera/Thinkstock.com; pp. 3-24 (text background), 5, 7, 17 iStockphoto/Thinkstock.com; p. 9 Vitaly Korovin/Shutterstock.com; p. 11 Stephen Hilger/Bloomberg/Getty Images; p. 13 Discovery FootageSource/Getty Images; p. 15 Jasmin Awad/Shutterstock.com; p. 19 Stocktrek Images/Getty Images; p. 21 © iStockphoto.com/photosbyjim.

Printed in the United States of America

CPSIA compliance information: Batch #CW14GS: For further information contact Gareth Stevens, New York, New York at 1-800-542-2595.

Contents

Words in the glossary appear in **bold** type the first time they are used in the text.

Ooh! Shiny!

Gold is like most other metals. It's malleable, which means it can be shaped without breaking it. It also carries, or conducts, electricity and heat. But not all metals are as valuable as gold. What makes gold so special?

Part of the reason is gold's appearance. All metals are shiny, but gold has a special glow, or luster, when it's **polished**. But perhaps what makes gold most valuable is how rare it is. Gold has been valuable to people throughout history.

METAL MANIA!

Gold is ductile. This means it can be stretched into wire. However, less costly metals like copper are usually used for wire.

For thousands of years, people have believed that gold is wealth. That's why gold and gold coloring are used to decorate buildings like this.

The Element Gold

Gold is an element. An element is a pure form of matter. It isn't mixed with any other matter. You can think of elements as building blocks that make up other kinds of matter. In fact, elements, including gold, make up the world around us.

Gold is found all over Earth, but in very small amounts. Some people guess that if all the gold found so far were melted down and shaped into a cube, it would measure just about 67 feet (20 m) on each side.

METAL MANIA!

The US Geological Survey guesses about 115,000 pounds (52,000 kg) of gold remain in the ground.

6

The Latin word for "gold" is *aurum*. Scientists sometimes refer to gold using a shortened form of the Latin name: Au.

7

Veins and Nuggets

Sometimes gold is found in "veins" within Earth's crust. Veins occur when heat from the planet's center, or core, forces hot liquid through cracks in the crust. The liquid carries water, bits of gold, other metals, and **minerals**. It cools and hardens into **ore**.

The gold in ore **deposits** can be as small as flakes or as big as nuggets. Gold is often found with the mineral quartz and the metals silver, copper, and iron. Forces of nature, such as flowing water, can carry gold away from a deposit.

METAL MANIA!

Veins are forming even today. Events like **earthquakes** can bring gold to Earth's surface.

Gold is heavy, so nuggets have been found at the bottom of rivers and streams. These finds aren't pure gold, though.

9

Gold Mines and Gold Fields

A gold **field** was discovered in South Africa in 1886. It's thought that 40 percent of all gold ever mined came from there. South Africa's Tau Tona Mine has the deepest tunnel on Earth. It goes 2.4 miles (3.9 km) below the surface! Workers in the tunnel have to watch out for harmful gases and other dangers.

If Nevada were a country, it would be fourth in total gold production. Northeast Nevada has the largest gold field in the United States. Eighty percent of US gold is mined there.

METAL MANIA!

The Tau Tona Mine gets hot—sometimes above 130°F (54°C).

10

In Nevada, gold ore is dug from the earth, producing huge open pits.

Pure Gold

Once ore is taken from the earth, the gold must be separated from the other matter. First, the ore is crushed. Water, **chemicals**, and the element carbon are added. Then, electricity is used to draw the gold bits together.

Next is the smelting process. The gold is melted, and more chemicals are added. It's hardened into bars, but it's not pure yet.

The last step is **refining** the gold. It's melted again, and any final **impurities** are removed. This gold may be 99.9 percent pure.

METAL MANIA!

Another way of removing gold from rock is letting certain kinds of **bacteria** eat the rock around the gold!

In the smelting process, gold is heated to more than 2,100°F (1,150°C).

13

Alloys

Gold is so soft it's usually combined with other metals to strengthen it. These mixtures of metals are called alloys. For jewelry, gold is often mixed with silver, zinc, or copper. Have you heard the term "24-karat gold"? This means the gold is as pure as it can be for jewelry. Fewer karats means less pure.

Gold is often recycled. If you have a gold necklace or ring today, it could have come from the gold jewelry worn by kings and queens of ancient times!

METAL MANIA!

About one-third of new gold products today come from gold that has been melted down and reshaped.

Without another metal added to it, gold jewelry is so soft it breaks easily.

15

Gold as Riches

Gold isn't used as money as it was in ancient days. It's used in jewelry, electronics, and as a way to store wealth. It's still worth a lot, but its value goes up and down. Governments also keep gold as a way to pay other countries.

The US government stores its gold in two locations: the Federal Reserve Bank in New York City and the **Bullion** Depository at Fort Knox, Kentucky. Walk into either place, and you'll see stacks of brick-like gold bars, known as ingots.

METAL MANIA!

Visitors aren't allowed in the Bullion Depository at Fort Knox, but you can see the gold in the Federal Reserve Bank in New York.

Each gold ingot at Fort Knox weighs 27.5 pounds (12.5 kg).

Gold in Business and Beyond

Gold is an important part of the business world. Electronics use gold because it conducts electricity so well. Most computers contain a few ounces of gold. Therefore, industries that use computers need gold as well, including NASA (National Aeronautics and Space Administration).

A thin layer of gold covers many parts of the International Space Station (ISS) to guard them from the sun's harmful rays and keep them from heating up. For the same reasons, **satellites** use gold as well.

METAL MANIA!

About 90 pounds (41 kg) of gold were used to make the space shuttle *Columbia*.

This supply pod for the ISS is covered in gold to keep it safe from the harsh conditions of space.

19

Gold in Weird Places!

You know about gold coins, wires, and jewelry, but gold can be found in some unusual places, too. Certain plants, such as alfalfa, collect gold from the soil in their roots as they take in water. Scientists wonder if this would be another way to mine the precious metal in the future!

Gold is nontoxic. That's why it's used in dental work. Gold is also in certain **medicines**. It's even found in some foods! Unsurprisingly, even the human body has a very small amount of gold.

METAL MANIA!

Perhaps $1 trillion of gold is waiting to be discovered in the world's oceans!

Could this alfalfa field be a gold field in the future?
We might be mining gold differently someday!

21

Glossary

bacteria: tiny creatures that can only be seen with a microscope

bullion: gold or silver in the form of bars

chemical: matter that can be mixed with other matter to cause changes

deposit: an amount of a mineral in the ground that built up over a period of time

earthquake: a shaking of the ground caused by the movement of Earth's crust

field: an area rich in a natural resource

impurity: something unwanted that is mixed in with a substance

medicine: a drug taken to make a sick person well

mineral: matter in the ground that forms rocks

ore: matter in the ground from which a metal can be removed

polish: to make something smooth and shiny by rubbing it with a soft cloth

refine: to make a purer form of something by removing unwanted substances

satellite: an object that circles Earth in order to collect and send information

For More Information

Books

Belval, Brian. *Gold*. New York, NY: Rosen Central, 2007.

Tocci, Salvatore. *Gold*. New York, NY: Children's Press, 2005.

Websites

All About Jewels: Gold
www.enchantedlearning.com/jewel/pages/gold.shtml
Learn about gold, gold alloys, and gold-related terms.

How Gold Works
www.howstuffworks.com/gold.htm
Read more about the history of gold, gold mining, and gold prospecting.

Story of Gold
www.gold.org/about_gold/story_of_gold/
Find gold facts, figures, and more on this site.

Index